PERSPECTIVES ON THE WORD OF GOD

PERSPECTIVES ON THE WORD OF GOD

AN INTRODUCTION TO CHRISTIAN ETHICS

JOHN M. FRAME

Wipf and Stock Publishers
150 West Broadway • Eugene OR 97401

1999

Perspectives on the Word of God
An Introduction to Christian Ethics

By Frame, John M.
Copyright©1999 by Frame, John M.

ISBN: 1-57910-257-3

Reprinted by *Wipf and Stock Publishers* 1999
150 West Broadway • Eugene OR 97401

Previously Published by Presbyterian & Reformed Publishing Co., 1990.

CONTENTS

PREFACE

The three chapters of this book consist of the Kenneth
Kantzer Lectures which I delivered at Trinity Evangelical
Divinity School on November 15 and 16, 1988.

I thought that this material might be a useful addition
to the other books I have written or have plans to write. My
Theology of Lordship series is proving to be a slower project
than I first envisioned. Though I am encouraged by the response to the first volume, *The Doctrine of the Knowledge of
God*, I'm a bit worried that the other books may be so slow in
coming that my friends will lose interest in the series! So in
the meantime, maybe this little book will help to bridge the

gap. It presents in brief some of the main theses from two of the forthcoming volumes, *The Doctrine of the Word of God* and *The Doctrine of the Christian Life*. I am hoping it will stimulate enough thought that perhaps some of you might share your responses with me so that I can work out my ideas more cogently in the larger volumes to come. The book may also be useful in that it presents some of my "perspectival" theses in much briefer form than in *Doctrine of the Knowledge of God*. It may therefore serve as a text in those courses wherein the teacher wants to give students a *taste* of my approach without going into enormous depth.

I wish to thank Trinity Evangelical Divinity School for their very gracious hospitality during the lecture series. I am also very pleased to honor, by the lectures and now the book, Dr. Kenneth Kantzer. For many years Dr. Kantzer has been a leader in theological education, first at Wheaton, now at Trinity. He has also been one of our leading Christian journalists, having been editor-in-chief of *Christianity Today* for several years and now as one of the senior editors of that magazine. I have especially enjoyed his editorial comments on the *Christianity Today* Institutes, of which he has served as Dean. His editorial writing seems to grow more interesting with each issue.

LECTURE
ONE

LECTURE ONE

THE NATURE OF
THE WORD OF GOD

INTRODUCTION TO THE LECTURE SERIES

I am very thankful to you for the invitation to speak here at Trinity. I've long respected the extraordinarily high level of scholarship among the faculty here and the strength of your stand for the authority of Scripture and for the evangelical gospel of salvation in Jesus Christ. I hope you will look to us at Westminster not only as academic colleagues, but also as comrades-in-arms in the battle for human lives and human society, as we seek to bring every thought captive to the obedience of Christ.

Before we get to our specific business for today, let me give you a brief overview of what I hope to accomplish in the entire series of three lectures. I gather that your invitation to me reflects some interest here in my book published about a year ago, called *The Doctrine of the Knowledge of God*.[1] In these lectures, therefore, I will be developing some of the ideas of that book—not simply repeating things I've said there, but making some fresh applications of the book's basic perspective. I hope to publish some of these fresh applications in later books and articles, and so I'm anxious to get your feedback during the question periods to help me with the formulations. By way of introduction, therefore, I will summarize some of the main ideas of the book, and then I will go on to the further developments I mentioned.

In *The Doctrine of the Knowledge of God* (or DKG) I attempted to develop a Christian epistemology or theory of human knowledge, based on the Bible. This project was based on the conviction that our God, through his word, desires to rule *all* aspects of human life—not only our worship and evangelism, not only what is usually described under the headings of personal and social ethics, but simply *everything*: "Whether you eat or drink or whatever you do, do it all for the glory of God" (I Cor. 10:31). This implies that even our scholarship, yes, all our thinking, must be uniquely Christian; it ought to be significantly different from the thinking of the non-Christian. I am not saying that we must disagree with everything that every non-Christian says. But even when we agree with the non-Christian, even when we hold views in common with him, there will still be a difference be-

1. Phillipsburg, N.J.: Presbyterian and Reformed, 1987.

tween us and him. In holding those common views, those agreements, we will have different goals, different motives, and we will be acknowledging different criteria.

So there is a distinctively Christian theory of knowledge, a view of human knowledge that is not shared with unbelievers.[2] The Christian may find himself agreeing at points with non-Christian philosophers, psychologists, geologists, and biologists, but he may never take such agreement for granted. He must constantly be on the alert to avoid the wrong turns of secular thought, even when those wrong turns may appear at first glance to be insignificant. God calls us to bring every thought captive to the obedience of Christ (II Cor. 10:5).

Therefore, in DKG I did not adopt a kind of Christianized variation on some secular theory or theories of knowledge. Rather, I began with Scripture and tried to determine what it says to us about matters epistemological. Of course, Scripture is not a treatise in epistemology, any more than it is a textbook of biology or auto repair. But I felt that my first responsibility, like the responsibility of the Christian biologist or auto repairman (repair-person?), was to determine what God had to say about my particular discipline. I could not, therefore, follow any of the main traditions of secular philosophy: rationalism, with its idolatry of the human intellect; empiricism, which adopts human sense-experience as its ultimate criterion of truth; or subjectivism, which denies the

2. An unbeliever may, of course, confess verbally a Christian theory of knowledge. The Pharisees were very orthodox in their beliefs but, Jesus teaches us, devoid of true faith. So a modern Pharisee might grant the truth of a Christian epistemology. But that would be contrary to the deepest inclinations of his heart, an inconsistency with his fundamental unbelief.

objectivity of truth altogether in favor of human feeling or inwardness. Nor was any combination of these acceptable for a Christian epistemology.

In a Christian theory of knowledge, God himself is the ultimate criterion of truth, and therefore his word to us, his revelation,[3] is the standard by which all truth claims must be judged. It is true, however, that we *apprehend* God's revelation by means of human reason, human sense-experience, and the whole range of hard-to-define intuitions, feelings, and consciousnesses we call "subjectivity." None of these, in itself, gives absolute knowledge. If it did, we would not need God's word. But these human faculties work together, in mutual dependence, to lead us toward that truth which is absolute and final, God's word to us.

DKG also explored some of the relations among these human faculties. God has set us free from trying to find an absolute authority or criterion within ourselves, and so we do not need to idolize human reason, sense-experience, or subjectivity. Thus we are set free to consider the possibility that these human faculties are *mutually* dependent. So I argue in that book what perhaps may appeal to your common sense, that reason, sense-experience, and subjectivity are dependent on one another, that they work together in producing human knowledge. Indeed, it might be better not to distinguish these

3. I prefer "word" to "revelation" as a broad designation for God's Creator-to-creature communication. I think that reflects the scriptural usage, in which "revelation" tends to be an eschatological or consummative category. There is a sense in which we do not now have "revelation" (cf. F. Gerald Downing, *Has Christianity a Revelation?* [Philadelphia: Westminster Press, 1964]), but we do have the word.

6

from one another in any rigid way. Rather, they should be as aspects of, or perspectives on, any human act of knowing.

Related to the distinction between reason, sense, and subjectivity is another threefold distinction that plays a major role in *DKG*. In any act of knowledge there are three crucial elements: (1) an object of knowledge, something that is known, (2) a subject of knowledge, the person who knows; and (3) a norm, criterion, or standard, by which we justify our claims to knowledge. In the book I argue that these three also are mutually dependent; none ever exists without the other two, and each may be defined in terms of the other two. The object and subject are what the law says they are. The norm and the subject are objects, facts to be known. And the object and norm are elements of subjective experience.

We can therefore look at any piece of human knowledge in three ways: (1) as a correspondence between idea and object, (2) as a state of warranted cognitive satisfaction in a subject, and (3) as human thinking that accords with God's laws for thought. In my technical vocabulary, to look at knowledge the first way is to look at it from the "situational perspective," the second from the "existential perspective," and the last from the "normative perspective."

In *DKG* I make a number of applications of this scheme, especially to apologetics. We can get some insight here, for instance, into the disagreement between presuppositionalism and evidentialism in apologetics. The presuppositionalist looks at apologetics primarily from the normative perspective, insisting that when we argue with the unbeliever, we must above all obey God's laws of thought, we must be faithful to the Lord. In that respect, I am emphatically a presuppositionalist. But the evidentialist has a point to make also, from the situational perspective. He says that we must offer evidence; we must be willing and able to show a correspondence between our theology and the real world. I gladly acknowledge that point, so you can call me an evidentialist as well as a presuppositionalist! I do not think those two insights are incompatible. On the contrary, I believe that they are both true and that they are both important to apologetics. They *appear* incompatible to some, because some people do not see the perspectival relation between the norm and the situation. And so I can also find some value in the "subjectivist" apologetics found in Pascal, Kierkegaard, and others, writers who tend to look at knowledge from the "existential perspective." I think John Calvin is also rather "existential" in his epistemology, but that's another story.

My final introductory point is that this threefold scheme is based ultimately upon the threefold relationship God himself sustains to the world. God is *Lord in Scripture* (*Yahweh*, *adon*, *kurios*). And his lordship involves at least three elements: (1) He is the Creator and *controller* of the world; he governs all "situations." (2) He is the rightful and ultimate *authority* over all his creatures. (3) As covenant Lord, he commits himself to his creatures, making them in his image, granting them inescapable knowledge of himself, entering relationships with them, making covenant promises, distributing blessing and judgment. As such, God is intimately *present*, personally involved with all aspects of his creatures' lives.

God's control is the source of our situational perspective: God makes the situation, the object of knowledge, to be what it is. His authority is the supreme norm of knowledge, making possible our human normative perspective. His presence is the source of our existential perspective, for it means

8

that we can find God's reality in the deepest recesses of ourselves as his image. God's control, authority, presence—these are, ultimately, the sources of all our knowledge.

Up to this point everything I've said is in *The Doctrine of the Knowledge of God* and is more fully developed there. In the remainder of this lecture, and in the two succeeding lectures, I intend, for the most part, to go beyond that book, hoping to show how the above framework is fruitful for other kinds of theological discussions. I have chosen here to focus on a topic closely related to the knowledge of God, namely the source of that knowledge in God's word. In my classes at Westminster Seminary, I deal with the word of God *before* I get into Christian epistemology, and I think that is the proper order. So in these lectures, I will be giving you a kind of "prequel" to *DKG*: a propaedeutic or introductory discussion that, nevertheless, is influenced by the epistemology presented in that book itself. The rest of this lecture will deal with the nature of the word of God. The second lecture will deal with the media of the word, the means by which God's word gets from him to us. The third lecture will deal with the role of the word in Christian ethics.

THE NATURE OF THE WORD OF GOD

What is the word of God? Most evangelicals would instinctively answer, "The Bible." And that answer naturally occurs to me as well. But as many theologians (not only liberals, but also evangelicals) will be quick to tell us, there are problems with any simple identification between the Bible and the word of God. Psalm 147, for instance, speaks this way:

9

He sends his command to the earth; his word runs swiftly. He spreads the snow like wool and scatters the frost like ashes. He hurls down his hail like pebbles. Who can withstand his icy blast? He sends his word and melts them; he stirs up his breezes, and the waters flow. (vv. 15-18)

Consider the difficulty of substituting "Bible" for "word" in that quotation. Or try substituting "Bible" for "word" in John 1:1, 14.

"Word of God" in Scripture, therefore, seems to have a broader meaning than "Bible." It describes the power by which God controls the forces of nature, and in some mysterious way it is also a name of God's eternal Son.

In order to be sufficiently broad, perhaps we must also be deliberately vague in our definition of the word of God. Let us say that the word is God's "self-expression," and then specify the various forms of self-expression that Scripture describes as divine speech.

1. First, the word of God is the *power* by which God brings all things to pass according to the counsel of his will (Eph. 1:11). It was by speech that God created the heavens and the earth (Gen. 1:3, 6; Pss. 33:6-9; 148:5; John 1:3; Heb. 11:3; II Pet. 3:5). God's providence is by speech—he commands, and things happen (Gen. 1:9, 11, 22; 8:21f.; Pss. 18:15; 28:3-9; 147:15-18; 148:5-8; Matt. 8:27). His judgments are also the outcome of his mighty voice (Gen. 3:14ff.; 6:7; 11:6f.; Ps. 46:6; Isa. 30:30; 66:6; Hos. 6:5; II Pet. 3:7; cf. Matt. 7:21-27; 25:31-46; esp. John 12:48). And his mercy also is a *word* of healing (Isa. 43:1; Luke 7:1-10; John 6:63, 68; Rom. 1:16; Phil. 2:16; I Tim. 1:10; I John 1:1), an "effectual calling" (Isa. 62:2; 65:15; Acts 2:39; Rom. 1:6f.; 8:28; I Cor. 1:2, 24, 26; Gal. 1:6; etc.).

10

There is nothing theologically new, of course, in the assertion that God's word is powerful; that was a point of discussion among the Protestant Reformers. The idea that the powers of God *in general* can be called "word" is harder to find in classic theology. But we should recall at this point the way especially the post-Reformation Calvinists spoke of God's "decrees" and "counsel." Following such passages as Luke 22:22; Acts 2:23; 4:28; and Eph. 1:11 these theologians spoke of all things taking place according to quasi-verbal acts of God called "decrees" or "counsels," thus making all events of nature and history to be the effects of God's words.

Oddly enough, those supreme anti-scholastics, those twentieth-century theologians who stressed the word of God while denying propositional revelation (such as Barth, Brunner, Bultmann), the theologians of the "new hermeneutic" (such as Ebeling and Fuchs), the "acts of God" theologians (such as G. Ernest Wright), and the "theology as history" school of Wolfhart Pannenberg—all of these, in varying ways, have echoed the decretalism of the seventeenth century. For they have seen the word of God essentially as a kind of power, an event, or as a force that makes things happen—not, to be sure, as an eternal decree, except perhaps in Barth; but as it were a kind of decree uttered in the present, in the here-and-now. Also, similar definitions of "word of God" can be found in the writings of the followers of Vollenhoven and Dooyeweerd, writers of orthodox Reformed background.[4]

---

4. For example, A. DeGraaff and C. Seerveld, eds., *Understanding the Scriptures* (Hámilton, Ontario: The Association for the Advancement of Christian Scholarship, 1968).

Nothing in Scripture requires the evangelical to disagree with the assertion that God's word is powerful and that God's powers are verbal. And it is certainly scriptural to say that God's word is a power, a force, or an event. It is not scriptural, however, to make the word *merely* a power, or to use the concept of power to *exclude* the dimension of propositional meaning. That is the mistake made by the thinkers listed in the previous paragraph, a mistake devastatingly rebutted in James Barr's 1966 work, *Old and New in Interpretation*.[5] We should, then, continue to search the Scriptures for other biblical characterizations of or "perspectives upon" the word of God.

2. The word of God is also God's *authoritative* speech. The difference between "power" and "authority" in my vocabulary (though not always in the English Bible) is that God's power determines what *will* happen, while God's authority determines what *ought to* happen. The distinction is the same as that in traditional theology between God's "decretive" and "preceptive" wills. That there is a difference between these, that God sometimes decrees to happen what his precepts forbid (see esp. Luke 22:22; Acts 2:23; 4:28), is the mystery, the stumbling block underlying the problem of evil in its various forms. My concern here, however, is not to solve those ancient mysteries, but simply to indicate that "word of God" in Scripture designates both the exertions of God's power and the expressions of God's authoritative will.

Throughout Scripture God speaks to human beings, setting forth his will for their lives. All the issues of life hinge on the human response to God's word. Adam's first recorded experience was that of hearing the word of God (Gen. 1:28ff.).

5. London: SCM Press, 1966.

His life or death depended on his response to that word (Gen. 2:17). After the fall, Adam's only hope was that God would fulfill the promise of his word (Gen. 3:15). Noah had no reason to believe divine judgment was imminent—except God's word. Abraham's faith, a model of Christian faith (Rom. 4; Gal. 3:6-9; Heb. 11:8-19; James 2:21-24), was faith in God's promise, his word. Israel under the Mosaic covenant was bound to the "laws," "statutes," "precepts," "commands," and "decrees" God had spoken (Deut. 6; Josh. 1:8f.; Ps. 119; Isa. 8:20; many other passages). Later, God spoke through the prophets (Deut. 18:15-22; Jer. 1:6-19; Ezek. 13:2f., 17). Then Jesus came, not to cancel the law, but to fulfill it (Matt. 5:17-20); and he gives us words of his own, which we need if we are to have life (Matt. 7:21ff., 28f.; Mark 8:38; Luke 8:21; 9:26ff.; John 6:63, 68; 8:47; 12:47ff.; 14:15, 21, 23f.; 15:7, 10, 14; 17:6, 17; I Tim. 6:3; I John 2:3-5; 3:22; 5:2f.; II John 6; Rev. 12:17; 14:12). The words of Jesus are the supreme test of discipleship. And the apostles claim that their words are on the same high level of authority (John 14:23-26; 15:26f.; 16:13; Rom. 2:16; 16:25; I Cor. 2:10-13; 4:1; II Cor. 4:1-6; 12:1, 7; Gal. 1:1, 11f., 16; 2:2; I Thess. 4:2; Jude 17f.).

No one can deny that according to Scripture the word of God is both power and intelligible content, or that that intelligible content functions as the supreme authority for human life. As Barr argued, however much we may wish as modern men to have a revelation of power without meaningful content, we cannot honestly claim that this modern viewpoint is the viewpoint of the Scriptures, Barth notwithstanding.

3. But third, the word of God is also God's *personal presence* with his creatures. Even in human language it is often difficult to separate a speaker from his words. If you are

thinking that my words are stupid, you are at the same time thinking that I am stupid. If you honor the words of Hemingway, to that extent you honor Hemingway. Language is quite central to human life (Prov. 12:18; 13:3; 18:20f.; 21:23; Matt. 12:34ff.; James 3:1-12), and important to human sin (Gen. 11:6; Pss. 12; 57:4; 64:3; 140:3; Prov. 10:19; 12:17-19; Isa. 29:13; Jer. 9:8; Ezek. 33:31; Rom. 3:13f.) and redemption (Ps. 51:15; Isa. 6; 35:6; 43:21; 45:23; 49:2; 65:19; Zeph. 3:9ff.; Rom. 10:9f.; James 5:16; I Pet. 2:9). Truly if one can control his tongue, he can control his whole life (James 3:1-12).

So it is difficult to separate God from his words. To obey his words is to obey God; to despise his words is to despise him. In many ways God's word is united with himself: (a) God's word reveals *him* (Deut. 4:5-8; II Tim. 3:15). (b) God's Spirit is present with his word (Gen. 1:2; Ps. 33:6; Isa. 34:16; 59:21; John 6:63; 16:13; Acts 2:1-4; I Thess. 1:5; II Thess. 2:2; II Tim. 3:16; II Pet. 1:21). (c) God's nearness is the nearness of the word (Deut. 4:5-8; 30:11-14; Rom. 10:6-8). (d) God's Ten Commandments were placed by the ark of the covenant in Israel, the holiest place of all, the most intense place of God's presence (Deut. 31:26). II Timothy 3:15 also refers to Scripture as "holy," recalling the Old Testament conviction that God's words partake of his own holiness. (e) All of God's acts are performed by speech, as we saw earlier under "power": his eternal plan, creation, providence, judgment, and grace. (f) God is distinguished from the idols by the fact that he speaks (I Kings 18:24, 26, 29, 36; Pss. 115:5ff.; 135:15ff.; Hab. 2:18-20; I Cor. 12:2). (g) The speech of God has divine attributes: it is wonderful (Ps. 119:129), eternal (Ps. 119:89, 160), omnipotent (Gen. 18:14; Isa. 55:11; Luke 1:37), perfect (Ps. 19:7ff.), holy (Deut. 31:26; II Tim. 3:15, cf. (*d*) above). (h) The word of God is an object of worship (Pss. 34:3; 56:4, 10; 119:48, 120, 161f.; Isa. 66:5). (Cf. the praising of God's *name*, Pss. 9:2; 68:4; 138:2; etc.)[6]

It should therefore not be too surprising for us to read in John 1:1 that "in the beginning was the word, and the word was with God, and the word was God." Of course this passage refers to the living word, Jesus Christ. But it is also relevant to the broader biblical doctrine of the word of God. "In the beginning" alludes to Genesis 1:1; that allusion is reinforced by the reference to creation in John 1:3. Therefore the word that was "with God" and "was God" was Jesus, and it was also the word that created the heavens and the earth. In some mysterious way Jesus, God, and the creative word are one. The doctrine of the Trinity itself can, perhaps, be helpfully formulated in linguistic terms (though of course not *only* in this way): God the Father is the one who speaks; the Son is the word spoken; the Spirit is that mighty breath (*ruah*, *pneuma*) that drives that word to accomplish its purpose.

All of this will remind us of the neoorthodox slogan that "God does not reveal propositions, he reveals himself." No doubt, God does reveal himself, and we ought to be humble enough to learn from the neoorthodox about that. They are surely wrong, however, to conclude that the self-revelation of God excludes meaningful content. Quite the contrary: that word which has divine attributes, which is an object of worship, which accompanies God in the very ark of the covenant is nothing more or less than the meaningful, authoritative word that God speaks to his people. Indeed Jesus himself, the supremely living word, comes with a *message*, a *gospel*.

6. Much could also be said about the union between the "name" of God and God himself, "name" and "word" being closely related concepts in Scripture: Exod. 33:19; 34:6f.; Ps. 7:17; etc.

We may sum up the nature of the word of God as follows; God's word is the self-expression of his lordship. His word is the expression of his control, authority, and presence —his self-insinuation into the three "perspectives" of human knowledge. The power of the word creates our situational perspective; the authority of the word determines the norms of our knowledge; and the presence of the word makes God inseparable from our self-knowledge.

LECTURE
TWO

LECTURE TWO

THE MEDIA OF
THE WORD OF GOD

In the previous lecture, I argued that God's word, according to Scripture, is the self-expression of God's lordship — of his control, his authority, and his presence.

But how does God's word get from him to us? That is the question of "media." All of God's word to us is mediated, in the sense that it always reaches us through some creaturely means. This is true even when revelation seems most "direct." For example, when God spoke to the people of Israel gathered around Mt. Sinai, and they heard the divine voice from heaven, even then God's word reached the people through creaturely media. For one thing, God spoke human language.

For another, he used the normal earthly atmosphere to transmit the sounds to the eardrums of the people. Further, it was the people's brain cells that interpreted the sounds as words and interpreted the words as God's message. God's word never lacks media when it is spoken to human beings.

DIVERSE KINDS OF MEDIA

What kinds of media are there? Well, here comes another threefold distinction. You may be thinking by now that these threefold distinctions are getting to be a little too schematic, too neat; I think so too, but I find them hard to avoid. Sometimes I think that I'm hooked into some mysterious trinitarian structure deep in Scripture; other times I think it's just a useful pedagogical device. Perhaps it all comes from sleeping through too many three point sermons as a child.

In any case, I will say that God reveals himself through events, words, and people. If you've been following me, you will see a rough correlation here with the previous triads (control-authority-presence and situational-normative-existential). When God reveals himself in events, he particularly displays his control, his power. When he reveals himself in words, he expresses his authority, his norms in a focused way. And when he reveals himself in people, he is obviously present with them in a profound way. At the same time, we should beware of making these correlations too precise. God's control is seen not only in event-revelation, but in revelation coming through all media. His authority is expressed not only in word revelation, but in all forms of revelation. And he is present not only when the medium is a person, but in all his speech.

Let us look more closely at the media.

1. EVENT-MEDIA

God reveals himself through what he *does* in our world. God's acts include the following.

a. Nature and general history (Gen. 9:12-17; Deut. 4:26; 30:19; 31:28; 32:1; Pss. 19; 46:8-10; 65; 104; 147:15-18; 148:5-8; Acts 14:17; 17:26-28; Rom. 1:18-32). Karl Barth to the contrary, God does reveal himself in the world as such — not only to believers, but to unbelievers as well — as the references in Acts and Romans indicate. Creation and providence do show that God exists, and they also reveal his character, his righteous standards for human life, and his holy wrath against human sin. Natural revelation is not itself a saving revelation. None of these texts indicates that someone could learn the gospel of grace from nature and general history alone. Rather, "Faith comes from hearing the message, and the message is heard through the word of Christ" (Rom. 10:17). But natural revelation does convey certain realities people must know if they are to understand and respond to the gospel.

b. Redemptive history (Exod. 14:31; 15; Deut. 8:11-18; Pss. 66:5-7; 135; 136; 145:4, 12; John 2:11; Acts 2 [esp. verse 22]; Rom. 1:4; Heb. 2:1-4; Rev. 15:3f.). God performs his "mighty acts" throughout redemptive history so that human beings may "know that I am the Lord." These are acts of both mercy and judgment. When Israel is delivered from Egypt, and the Egyptian army is destroyed, both Israel and Egypt come

21

to know that God is Lord. In these actions he demonstrates the attributes of lordship: his control, his authority, and his presence.

c. *Miracle*. The miraculous is perhaps a subset of the previous category, though some scriptural language suggests that the two categories are identical. All of God's acts of redemption and judgment, whether within or beyond "natural law" in our modern reckoning, are "signs," "wonders," "powers." At any rate, miracle, like redemptive history in general, displays God's lordship in terms of his control (*dunamis*), his authority (*semeion*), and his awesome presence (*teras*).

My category of event-media is not quite the same as the traditional concept of "general revelation." If we are to divide all revelation into "general" and "special," I would have to say that redemptive history and miracle are in the "special" category. This indicates, perhaps, that we need more distinctions than the traditional categories provide.

2. WORD-MEDIA Gods Self expression through human word

God also reveals himself by speaking in human-words. Notice that at this point I am beginning to speak of the "word of God" in a second sense. Originally, I defined "word of God" as the self-expression of God's lordship. In that sense, the word of God is expressed in all media. Now we can use "word of God" also in a somewhat narrower sense: a self-expression of God's lordship delivered to us through a particular kind of medium — human words.

As I mentioned earlier in connection with James Barr's argument, it is unscriptural to represent revelation as taking place only through events and not through words. Review

δυναμυς τερας
δεμgOv

the passages mentioned earlier in connection with God's "authority" in revelation. To Adam, Noah, Abraham, and so on, God spoke *words* that carry the authority of his lordship.

It will be edifying for us to distinguish several types of word-media:[1]

a. *The divine voice.* In some biblical instances God speaks "directly" to people. Under this category I would include God's utterances at Mount Sinai (Exod. 19; 20), at the transfiguration of Christ (Luke 9:35), before his passion (John 12:28), and at other times (Gen. 1:28ff.; 2:16; etc.). God's words *to* the prophets would be in this category, but not his words *through* them, which we will mention later. All the words of Jesus during his earthly ministry would be in this category.

I put quotes around the term "directly" above because, as I indicated earlier, no revelation of God to us is "purely" direct. Even the divine voice is mediated to its hearers by the wind currents, the hearer's brain cells, etc. Also, it should be noted that the divine voice speaks a human language and thus places itself under the limitations of what that language can express. In the divine voice, God "accommodates" himself to his hearers, lisps with them as Calvin says. One may say that even when God speaks with his own lips, not the lips of a prophet, there is still a "human element" in his communication.

Nevertheless, this accommodation does not diminish in any way the authority with which God speaks (or, indeed, the power and presence of his word). Who among us, when

1. For a fuller treatment of these distinctions, see Wayne Grudem, "Scripture's Self-Attestation," in D. A. Carson and John Woodbridge, eds., *Scripture and Truth* (Grand Rapids: Zondervan, 1983), especially 19-27.

confronted by the divine voice, would dare to disobey it? God's people are under obligation to obey all the words that proceed from his mouth.

b. *God's word through the prophets and apostles.* When God speaks through prophets and apostles, there is, we might say, even more "accommodation." In the prophetic word, God speaks not only in human language, but through a human messenger. Nevertheless, it is clear that what the prophet says is nothing less than God's very word. A prophet is one who has God's word in his mouth (Exod. 4:10-16; Deut. 18:15-22; Jer. 1:6-19). The religious veneration offered to the word of God in the Psalms is directed toward the word of God given through Moses (Pss. 12; 19:7ff.; 119). An apostle is one whom Jesus appointed to bring his gospel to the world (John 14:23-26; 15:26f.; 16:13). The apostles claim a divine source for their message (I Cor. 2:10-13; 4:1; Gal. 1:1, 11f., 16; 2:2; Eph. 3:3). Paul's word is the test of anyone who claims to be a prophet or "spiritually gifted" (I Cor. 14:37).

c. *God's written word.* The writing of revelation is not a merely incidental feature of its history. From the very beginning God had a specific purpose for the writing of revelation, and he authorized that writing explicitly. Meredith G. Kline's *The Structure of Biblical Authority*[2] argues cogently, in my opinion, that the writing of revelation corresponds to the ancient custom of producing official documents as witnesses to suzerainty treaties, what Scripture calls "covenants." However we may evaluate Kline's correlation of written revelation

2. Grand Rapids: Eerdmans, 1972.

with extrabiblical customs, Scripture itself leaves no doubt that God is the author of the written revelation.

The Ten Commandments, written on stone tablets, are identified as the covenant between God and his people (Exod. 34:28; Deut. 9:9, 11, 15). In them, God speaks as the author: "I am the Lord your God, who brought you out of Egypt, out of the land of slavery" (Exod. 20:2). Not only is God the literary author, he is also the publisher. The Ten Commandments are "tablets of stone inscribed by the finger of God" (Exod. 31:18; cf. 24:12; 32:15f.; 34:1; Deut. 4:13; 9:10f.; 10:2-4). Although Moses himself played a role in the production of the tablets (Exod. 31:18; Deut. 31:24), it is clear that God is regarded as the author of the words *in their written form*. Other words of Moses (Deut. 31:24-29) and later of Joshua (Josh. 24:25f.) were added to the decalogue and placed beside it near the holy ark, identifying those words also as words of God and establishing a pattern for the future development of the canon. The New Testament, in such familiar passages as Matthew 5:17-20; John 10:33-36; II Timothy 3:15-17; II Peter 1:19-21, attests the identity of the entire Old Testament with God's written word.[3]

It is clear that from the beginning of Israel's existence as a people (and perhaps even before that, as the "books of generations" in Genesis may attest) God has desired to rule his people by a book, a written constitution. The concept of a written word of God, bearing the full authority of God, is not

---

3. The exegetical case is well made by many evangelical writers such as Wayne Grudem in the article mentioned earlier. B. B. Warfield's *The Inspiration and Authority of the Bible* (Philadelphia: Presbyterian and Reformed, 1964) continues to be an important source in this regard.

a product of twentieth-century fundamentalism, or seventeenth-century rationalism, or medieval scholasticism, or post-apostolic defensiveness, or pharisaic legalism. It is embodied in the very constitution of the people of God and is assumed throughout Scripture. Modern theologians have opposed this idea by saying that the word of God is too transcendent or too dynamic to be kept in a book. Barth argued on such grounds that revelation cannot be "preserved." But in Scripture God explicitly calls upon his people to preserve the word from one generation to another (Deut. 6:6ff.; Jude 3). There is a "tradition," a permanent "body of truth" to be handed down (I Cor. 15:2f.; II Thess. 2:15; 3:6; I Tim. 6:20; II Tim. 1:12ff.; 2:2; II Pet. 2:21).[4]

And there is certainly no difference in authority among the divine voice, the prophetic word, and the written word. Almost every page of Deuteronomy contains admonitions to obey all the "statutes," "ordinances," "testimonies," "words," "commandments," "decrees," "stipulations," or "laws" (all that rich redundancy!) that are *written* in the law of Moses. The religious reverence given to the word of God in Psalms 19:7ff.; 119 and elsewhere is directed toward the *written* word of God, the statutes and ordinances made known through Moses. Like all forms of the word, the written word deserves the honor that belongs to God himself.

Nor can it be argued that although the Old Testament is a "religion of the book" or a "religion of the word," the New Testament is a wordless "religion of the spirit." Certainly the

---

4. On the question of the transcendence of God's word, see my "God and Biblical Language" in John W. Montgomery, ed., *God's Inerrant Word* (Minneapolis: Bethany Fellowship, 1974).

New Testament describes an unprecedented outpouring of God's Spirit upon his people, which exposes the inadequacy of any legalistic religion (II Cor. 3:6). But as we have already seen, Jesus gave to his disciples, and the apostles gave to the church, words revealed by God, words by which we live or die. Where are those words to be found? If they are lost in history, then the Christian faith itself, indeed our eternal life, is lost in history; and we who hoped to be saved by Christ are of all human beings most miserable. If these words are accessible only to scholars, then eternal life itself is accessible only to scholars and to those willing to bow before the authority of such scholars. If they are to be found in oral tradition or church dogma, the question is *Which* oral tradition or *which* church dogma? If they come by a revelation of the spirit given individually to each person, then how are they to be recognized, to be distinguished from fantasy or wishful thinking? And how, then, is the gospel to be preached publicly? But of course all of those alternatives, common though they be in modern theology, really deny what God has promised us: words of life, words on which we can rely for our eternal salvation, words we can pass along to our children and our children's children.

Where, then, are those words to be found? Is it too much to expect that, as with the Old Testament, the New Testament words of life would be located in a book? Surely from what we have seen so far, there is nothing about written words to make them unworthy of God. God has already shown us that he *likes* to speak to human beings through written words. He prefers, indeed, not to speak to each person individually, though he is quite capable of doing that, but rather to speak publicly, to spread his speech out on the public record so that all alike can come and see. He prefers to place his words in a written constitution so that a *people* may be formed, a *body* of individuals, visibly and externally (as well as invisibly and internally) united and governed by their allegiance to a particular text. And he speaks through that text, as we have seen, with the same authority as the divine voice itself.

Yes, we should expect this; and indeed, this is what God provides for us in the New Testament. In the nature of the case, the evidence for the existence of a New Testament canon is more subtle than the corresponding evidence concerning the Old Testament because the New Testament logically could not, prior to its completion, refer to itself as a finished canon. But the apostles certainly do present their written words as having all the authority of their spoken words (I Cor. 14:37; II Pet. 3:16; cf. Col. 4:16; I Thess. 5:27; II Thess. 3:14; I Tim. 5:18; see traditional evangelical exegetical treatments of these texts). Their words are included in that "deposit" of faith which we are to guard and to pass along to later generations.[5]

The written words of God are (perhaps with the exception of the first tablets of the decalogue, which were "written by the finger of God") also written by human authors. Much has been said about the relation of the divine to the human author, and no doubt much remains to be said. Hermeneutical problems abound here, which I will not seek to address.[6] But

5. On the question of the transmission of the text, the question of whether and how the *copies* of Scripture can be authoritative, see Greg L. Bahnsen, "The Inerrancy of the Autographa," in N. Geisler, ed., *Inerrancy* (Grand Rapids: Zondervan, 1979).

6. This has been done well in many evangelical volumes, such as *Hermeneutics, Authority, and Canon*, eds. D. A. Carson and John D. Woodbridge (Grand Rapids: Zondervan, 1986).

it is important to remember that whatever problems need to be addressed, however the human authors are to be fitted into the equation, it is not wrong to look at these writings simply as the word that God has written to us. Any epistemology or hermeneutic that casts doubt upon the authority, clarity, or sufficiency of God's written words is to that extent itself questionable.

 d. Preaching. What of preaching as a form of the word of God? We recall that Karl Barth regarded preaching as a form of revelation subordinate to Christ and to Scripture. The Second Helvetic Confession (I, iv) says that "the preaching of the word of God is the word of God." Certainly that was true of the preaching of the prophets and apostles. What of preachers today? Scripture doesn't comment directly on this question, but we may apply some broader biblical principles to it. Surely, on the one hand, if I am right about the written word as the constitution of the church, we cannot put preaching today on the same level as that constitution. If we do, the constitution loses its unique authority; sermons become as important and as authoritative as Scripture. It is, therefore, important to make a distinction between inspired and noninspired speech. The Bible is inspired (*theopneustos*, II Tim. 3:16), but today's sermons are not. In that sense, preaching is not the word of God. On the other hand, authentic preaching always seeks to set forth not the preacher's ideas, but the Scriptures. Insofar as the preacher *succeeds* at presenting not his own ideas, but God's, then surely there is a sense in which his sermon is the word of God. After all, God's word does not lose its authority merely by being placed on the lips of a human preacher, any more than it loses authority by being

29

set on paper. Indeed, we may say that preaching, when it is *true* preaching, when it is *authentic* preaching, is the word of God, nothing less. Take heed how you hear! You may not shrug off the biblical message simply because it comes from a human being, perhaps from a preacher you don't like very much. The word of God on his lips is God's word to you.

3. PERSON-MEDIA

God also reveals himself through persons. This type of revelation, like the others, occurs in various forms:

a. The human constitution. We are made in the image of God, and, whatever that means, it means at least that we *are* revelation. It would not be scriptural to say that we "are" the word of God, or that the events of nature and history (category 1, above) "are" the word of God; only "word revelation" in the narrow sense, revelation through word-media (category 2, above), can be *identified* with the word of God. But the word of God is *made known* through each of us.

Theologies differ as to whether the image of God was lost following Adam's fall. With the Reformed tradition generally, I hold that the image remains (Gen. 5:1; 9:6; I Cor. 11:7; James 3:9), though it is defaced, marred by human sin. God restores that image to believers through Christ (Eph. 4:24; Col. 3:10) so that we become more and more like him. But even unbelievers cannot escape the revelation of God in their own persons, any more than they can escape God's revelation in the facts of creation external to them. God's reality is stamped on every fact; it is found wherever we look, outward or inward.

b. *The example of Christian leaders.* Leadership, in Scripture, is based primarily upon spiritual maturity (I Tim. 3:1-13; Titus 1:6-9), as well as upon teaching ability and doctrinal soundness. A leader is not to teach only with words, but also with his life, to be a particular reflection of Jesus Christ. He is to be capable of "imitation" (I Cor. 4:16; 11:1; Phil. 3:17; I Thess. 1:6; 2:6; II Thess. 3:7-9; Heb. 13:7). Not only the apostles, but all leaders are to be godly examples to the flock (I Thess. 1:7; I Tim. 4:12; Titus 2:7; I Pet. 5:3).

There is something very significant here. Important as is the written word as the constitution of the church, it is insufficient in itself to meet all the needs of God's people. Note the interesting "travelogue" sections of Paul's epistles. Over and over again Paul expresses a desire to address the churches not only by letter, but also in person (Rom. 1:8-17; 15:14-33; I Cor. 4:14-21; 5:1-5; II Cor. 7:5-16; 12:14-13:10; Gal. 4:12-20; Eph. 6:21f.; Col. 4:7ff.; I Tim. 3:14f.; II Tim. 4:6-18; Titus 3:12- 14; Heb. 13:7f., 22f.; II John 12; III John 13). (I have enumerated these verses at length to indicate the pervasiveness of this theme, which rather surprised me when I first began to study it.) Paul's personal presence adds something not found in the written word as such. There is something about Paul's personal presence that adds credibility to his words.

c. *The presence of God himself.* God reveals himself also by presenting his own person before us. In Scripture, we find this revelation in theophany, God's assuming visible form to meet with human beings (Gen. 16:7ff.; 21:17ff.; Exod. 23:31; Isa. 6:1ff.; etc.). But in addition to theophany, God "meets" with us in all of the previously mentioned forms of revelation. When God speaks to his people, even if there is no visible form (Deut. 4:15), he is surely there. When God speaks through preachers and teachers, his Spirit accompanies the word to achieve his purpose (Jer. 1:12; I Thess. 1:5). The written word is the product of God's Spirit (I Cor. 2:13; II Tim. 3:16).

The idea of God's personal presence in revelation leads us immediately to think of Jesus Christ, the living word of God (John 1:1). Jesus mediates all other forms of God's word (Matt. 11:25-28; John 14:6). He is the author of God's revelation in creation and providence (John 1:3, 10; I Cor. 8:6; Col. 1:16; Heb. 1:2). He is the content of the Scriptures (Luke 24:25-27; John 5:45-47; I Cor. 10:4), the ultimate prophet (Luke 4:17-21; John 3:34ff.; 5:20; 7:16; 8:28; 12:47-49; 17:8; 19:24, 31; Acts 3:22f.; 7:37), the ultimate example (Matt. 11:29; 16:24; John 13:35; I Cor. 11:1; I Pet. 2:21; I John 3:16). Thus we may say that God—Jesus!—is present whenever God speaks to people.

THE UNITY OF THE WORD OF GOD

In the foregoing discussion I have enumerated the various "media" of God's word under the categories of events, words, and persons. Those distinctions are useful, I think, for analysis and for correlation with the "lordship triad" of control, authority, and presence. It would be wrong, however, to separate these sharply from one another.

From one point of view, we can say that some of God's revelations are events, some words, some manifestations of his personal presence. The parting of the Red Sea (or Sea of Reeds, or whatever) was an event-revelation. The two tables of the Decalogue were word-revelation. The coming of the Spirit at Pentecost was a manifestation of God's personal presence.

But in another sense we cannot neatly distinguish these forms of revelation. The parting of the Red Sea is, for us, a part of written Scripture; and, of course, it was a sign of the presence of the Lord in his creation. The two tables of the Decalogue were word-revelation, but their promulgation was a redemptive event, in the context of other redemptive events, in which God was clearly present. And the coming of the Spirit is also a redemptive event, described and interpreted in Holy Scripture.

Even general or natural revelation is a mark of God's presence (Rom. 1:18) and cannot *rightly* be used unless it is correlated with the word of the gospel. Apart from faith in Christ, there will always be some suppression of the truth, an exchange of the truth for a lie (Rom. 1:25).

The right use of each form of revelation requires the use of the others. (1) I need Scripture and the Spirit rightly to interpret creation. (2) I need the objective revelation of Scripture and creation to "test the spirits." (3) I need a spirit-led understanding of creation to *apply* Scripture to the situations in which I find myself. So understanding one form of revelation involves understanding all forms of it. Our understanding grows not by looking at the forms of revelation in isolation from one another, but by constantly correlating them, comparing them, and viewing them together.

So the three sets of media are not three different groups of revelations. Rather, they are three perspectives on a single unified revelation of God. We can look at that revelation as (1) a series of events, described in Spirit-attested Scripture, to which we must respond in faith; (2) spoken and written words attested by the spirit, describing God's mighty acts, which call for us to answer; (3) a person, calling us to himself in Scripture and experience. It is wrong to set these over against one another or to deny one in the interest of maintaining others. Revelation is an organic unity.

THE WORD OF GOD
AND THE KNOWLEDGE OF GOD

The moral of these two lectures is that although "word of God" in Scripture means something more than "Bible," and modern theologians are right in drawing our attention to the historical and the personal dimensions of God's speech, still the Holy Scriptures play an absolutely crucial role in the overall organism of revelation, as the covenant constitution of the people of God. It is possible for an evangelical to be a "biblicist" in the sense that he or she, purposefully or not, tends to ignore event- and person-revelation; and we should be humble enough to accept such criticism, even from liberals, when it is rightly due. But it is also possible to be a "historicist," looking only at "event-revelation," and looking at it without the guidance of Scripture and the Spirit. Such a historicist will deny what Spirit-attested Scripture says about history. Or one may be a "mystic," absorbed in the revelation given by the Spirit to our subjectivity, but ignoring Scripture and creation. But none of these positions—biblicism, historicism, or mysticism—so understood, is biblically defensible. If evangelicals have sometimes erred in the biblicist direction, certainly nonevangelicals have erred more often in the directions of historicism and mysticism. We should seek to avoid biblicism without falling into the other traps.

And thus we see also how God's word insinuates itself into human knowledge. Our situational, normative, and existential perspectives are profoundly affected by God's word. (1) Because God's word is event, it has radically influenced the situation in which we live. Nature and history are what they are because God has acted on and in them. (2) Because God's word is word, it sets forth clearly the norms for human thought and life. (3) Because God's word is his person, and because his word is manifested in our own persons, he confronts us throughout our own subjectivity. God's revelation, therefore, is truly inescapable. One cannot think adequately about anything without taking God into account. The rationalist cannot escape because God is the inescapable norm for human reason. The empiricist cannot escape because God is the supreme fact of experience. The subjectivist cannot escape because his very subjectivity points to God. But when the believer meditates on all of this, the omnipresence of God begins to take on new meaning.

> Underneath me, all around me, is the current of thy love;
> Leading onward, leading homeward, to thy glorious rest
> above.[7]

---

7. Samuel T. Francis, "O the Deep, Deep Love of Jesus," Copyright by Pickering and Inglis, Ltd.

LECTURE THREE

LECTURE
THREE

THE WORD OF GOD
AND CHRISTIAN ETHICS

In the previous two lectures I have discussed the nature and the media of the word of God, using the triperspectival categories of my book *The Doctrine of the Knowledge of God*[1] to unpack some of the distinctions Scripture makes at least implicitly. In this lecture I turn to the human use of the word of God, specifically in making ethical decisions. Rather than discussing specific ethical problems, I will be presenting a "meta-ethic," or a general method for approaching ethical problems. This method does not provide a simple, automatic

1. Phillipsburg, N.J.: Presbyterian and Reformed, 1987.

solution for all our ethical dilemmas. Indeed, part of its value is that it shows us why ethical problems are often so difficult. Still, it does provide us with some Christian guidelines that we need to follow if we are to make any progress at all in finding solutions.

I have presented the most basic features of this meta-ethic in my recently published *Medical Ethics: Principles, Persons, and Problems.*[2] I have also alluded to it in *The Doctrine of the Knowledge of God,* which applies the same general scheme to epistemology. Although my epistemology was published before my ethics, I developed the threefold scheme in ethics before applying it to epistemology. Ethics is its natural home, and I think the ethical applications of it are more easily understood than the applications to epistemological theory. Indeed the point of my epistemology is that epistemology can be fruitfully understood as a subdivision of ethics and thus can be fruitfully analyzed by the use of my meta-ethic. But although I have described this meta-ethic elsewhere, I intend here to present it in more detail than I have before, with some comparisons and ramifications that I have not discussed in published materials. Particularly I would like to compare this approach with those of secular philosophical ethical systems.

THREE SECULAR ETHICAL PHILOSOPHIES

The history of secular philosophical ethics presents us with three (there's that number again!) meta-ethical tenden-

2. Phillipsburg, N.J.: Presbyterian and Reformed, 1988.

cies. I say "tendencies" rather than "positions," because most ethical writers reflect more than one; rarely does anyone seek to be a pure representative of one or another. Let me name them as they have sometimes been named by others: existential, teleological, and deontological.

1. EXISTENTIAL ETHICS

Existential ethics is the view that ethics is essentially a matter of human inwardness, a matter of character and motive. Ethical behavior, on this view, must not be motivated by external reward, which would be mercenary, or by mere law, which would be drudgery. Either of these would also be hypocrisy, for in these cases people do things they would prefer not to do—for the sake of something outside themselves—masking their true character and therefore masking their true ethical state. Rather, ethical behavior is an expression of what a person is. One ought not to mask his nature; rather he should act it out. He should be what he is. There is no standard outside ourselves; what values there are in the world are the results of our decisions.

The existential tendency can be found in the Greek sophists,[3] who denied the existence of objective truth but

3. My comments on the history of ethics are not particularly original. I owe much to sources such as Frank Thilly and Ledger Wood, *A History of Philosophy* (New York: Henry Holt, 1951), Alasdair MacIntyre, *A Short History of Ethics* (New York: Macmillan, 1966), and Paul Edwards, ed., *The Encyclopedia of Philosophy* (New York: Macmillan and The Free Press, 1967). My purpose is to take *standard* criticisms of various secular ethicists and to show that those standard criticisms form a pattern that invites Christian interpretation and evaluation. For that purpose, I believe that to produce truly original critiques of these figures would be counterproductive.

sought to teach young people how to accomplish their own ambitions. It is also found in the Socratic "know thyself" and the Aristotelian-Thomistic concept of self-realization or self-actualization.[4] The Hegelians also emphasized self-realization.[5] The modern existentialist Jean Paul Sartre offered a self-realization ethic without the self.[6] Since he denied the existence of any objective human nature, he argued that ethical behavior was at best an expression of human *freedom*, of our *difference* from all things with objective natures. Sartre's view would be the purest philosophical form of "existential" ethic, but one suspects that there are many nonphilosophers who hold, in effect if not in word, such a view. For those who have become epistemological skeptics or, worse, have come to despair of all values, there is no very plausible form of ethics except existentialism.

Nonexistentialists have appreciated and sometimes appropriated the existentialist emphasis upon the inner life, upon good motives as the source of right action. Indeed, this emphasis echoes the biblical teaching that out of the heart are the issues of life (Prov. 4:23; cf. 29:13). Jesus taught that from the heart comes human speech (Matt. 12:34), true forgiveness (Matt. 18:35), true love (Mark 12:30, 33), as well as all other ethical good and evil (Matt. 15:19; Luke 6:45; 8:15; 16:15;

4. Aristotle, *Nicomachean Ethics* in R. McKeon, ed., *The Basic Works of Aristotle* (New York: Random House, 1941), 935-1127.

5. For example, F. H. Bradley, *Ethical Studies* (Oxford: Oxford University Press, 1876).

6. See his *Being and Nothingness*, trans. Hazel Barnes (New York: Methuen, 1957) and his summary article, "Existentialism Is a Humanism," in W. Kaufmann, ed., *Existentialism From Dostoyevsky to Sartre* (New York: Meridian, 1956).

Acts 5:3). But when, as in Sartre, the existentialist tendency reaches the point of denying objective, external value, many resist. This sort of skepticism is always self-refuting, for in it the denial of value is presented as a value, the denial of truth as a truth. Sartre, indeed, proposes a human lifestyle that he describes as "authentic." But what is that, if it is not an objective value?

2. TELEOLOGICAL ETHICS

Many who cannot accept the skepticism of existential ethics are attracted to teleological ethics, which affirms the existence of objective values to some extent. The term "teleological" is from the Greek *telos*, which means end or goal. The teleologist sets forth one relatively simple, objective goal for ethics, which, he thinks, no human being can legitimately question. That goal is usually called "happiness" or "pleasure." Teleologists, then, seek to evaluate all human behavior in terms of what it contributes to happiness or pleasure. This procedure seems to them to be practical and reflects the way many nonphilosophical people make ethical judgments.

Teleological ethics is frequently linked to an empiricist theory of knowledge. The empiricist thinks he can show by sense experience that everyone naturally seeks pleasure or happiness. Once that is granted, he presents another argument from sense experience to show the best means of attaining pleasure or happiness.

Aristotle's ethic has teleological elements (as well as elements of the other two tendencies).[7] More consistently

---

7. Aristotle, *Nichomachaen Ethics.*

teleological were the Greek Cyrenaics and Epicureans.[8] The best-known modern teleologists have been the nineteenth-century utilitarians Jeremy Bentham[9] and John Stuart Mill.[10] Most of us, indeed, find ourselves arguing ethical issues this way at times: what legislative policy, we often ask, will bring the greatest good for the greatest number? That is teleological ethics. Indeed, one might say that democracy is biased in favor of teleological ethics; for the voting process (and to a great extent also the Gallup-type poll) gives people frequent means of expressing to their representatives their degree of happiness. Arguments about what is right, therefore, often are resolved into arguments about what will make people happy, and that question in turn becomes the question of what people will vote for, or what pollsters think the people want.

Most reflective people will agree with Bentham and Mill that ethics is goal-oriented, that it seeks means of attaining goals we find valuable. Beyond that, however, many have found problems in teleological ethics. For one thing, the teleologists disagree among themselves as to precisely what

8. For readings in these schools, see T. V. Smith, ed., *Philosophers Speak for Themselves: From Aristotle to Plotinus* (Chicago: University of Chicago Press, 1934).

9. See his *An Introduction to the Principles of Morals and Legislation* (New York: Hafner, 1948; originally published 1823).

10. See his *Utilitarianism*, reprinted often, most interestingly found in a volume of the Encyclopedia Brittanica's *Great Books of the Western World* entitled *American State Papers* (Chicago, 1952). The volume also contains the Declaration of Independence, the Constitution, and Mill's works on democracy, *On Liberty* and *Representative Government*. I may be reading too much into this, but it is interesting that Brittanica has included utilitarian ethics as among the foundational principles of U.S. politics.

the goal is. Is it individual pleasure (Epicurus) or the pleasure of society in general (Mill)? Is pleasure to be measured by mere intensity (Cyrenaics, Bentham), or are there also qualitative judgments to be made (Epicurus, Mill)?

Further, what basis is there for saying that pleasure is the goal of human life? This is not, contrary to many teleologists, a simple empirical question. Nietzsche, for instance, denied that human beings pursue pleasure above all other goals; he thought that power was more fundamental than pleasure as a goal of human life. How would we settle this kind of disagreement? And even if we agree with Mill that human beings naturally seek pleasure for themselves, what proof is there that they seek it for society in general ("the greatest pleasure for the greatest number")? And even if we grant that human beings do naturally seek the happiness of society, how can we prove, as the teleologist must, that they *ought* to do so? Teleologists have never succeeded in satisfying their critics on these points.

Indeed, some have criticized the principle of "the greatest happiness for the greatest number" as a wicked idea. Might not a racist nation one day derive its maximum happiness from inflicting terrible cruelties upon a despised minority? Teleological ethics seems far too open to the principle that the end justifies any means whatsoever.

And for good measure, even if we grant "happiness" as a social goal, how do we calculate the means of attaining it? To calculate that we must seek the causes of universal happiness, through a possibly infinite period of future history encompassing the whole universe. But who knows what effects any human action may have over such a wide stretch of space and time? And there are so many different kinds of pleasure

45

and pain! What computer would be capable of taking all these data and problems into consideration?

3. DEONTOLOGICAL ETHICS

The third tendency is toward "deontological ethics," or an ethic of duty. Deontologists realize that objective moral standards are hard to find on either an existential or a teleological basis. They frankly admit that no such standards can be found either in human subjectivity (as in existentialism) or in empirical knowledge (as in teleological approaches). But they believe that objective ethical standards, absolute duties, can be found in some other way, and that one may define proper ethical behavior simply as the fulfillment of those duties.

In their view, a truly righteous person does not do his duty out of personal inclination (as in existentialism) or out of some calculation of happiness (as in teleological systems). Rather, a good will is one with which a person does his duty "for duty's sake," as Kant put it. A duty is self-attesting and, as such, supremely authoritative; it doesn't need to be recommended on the basis of some supposedly more ultimate consideration. We should not do our duty to get rewards, or to please other people, or to become happier, or to achieve self-realization, but simply because duty is duty, because it is moral law.

Plato's thoughts about ethics were probably more deontological than anything else, though not purely so. His "Idea of the Good" is a kind of self-attesting value that transcends all others and is known in a nonempirical way.[11] More con-

11. See various Platonic dialogues dealing with ethical matters, such as *Gorgias*, *Euthyphro*, and *Republic* (esp. chap. 23). See, e.g., Edith Hamilton and Huntington Cairns, eds., *The Collected Dialogues of Plato* (Princeton: Princeton University Press, 1961).

sistent, though less profound, were the ethical systems of the Cynics and Stoics, who both urged their hearers to renounce the supremacy of pleasure.[12] In more recent times, Immanuel Kant[13] is the most famous deontologist, flanked by David Hume[14] and G. E. Moore,[15] who developed influential arguments against teleological ethics, specifically arguments against trying to prove moral principles empirically. Hume argued that "you cannot reason from 'is' to 'ought,'" you cannot reason from a factual state of affairs to a conclusion stating an ethical value or obligation. Moore called this sort of argument "the naturalistic fallacy." And if teleological ethics is guilty of the naturalistic fallacy, and if existentialist ethics are otherwise objectionable, it would then seem that we should choose a deontological alternative.

Most writers since Moore have accepted, in general, his account of the naturalistic fallacy. The broader concern of deontologism—for having a system of absolute duties—is also appreciated by many who seek to get beyond the popular relativism and ethics-by-Gallup-poll of our present day. There is, especially since C. S. Lewis's influential article "The Humanitarian Theory of Punishment,"[16] a greater willingness among

12. See T. V. Smith, ed., *Philosophers Speak for Themselves* for readings in these movements.

13. See *Foundations of the Metaphysics of Morals*, in Brendan Liddell, ed., *Kant on the Foundations of Morality* (Bloomington and London: Indiana University Press, 1970).

14. See especially the last paragraph of Part I, Section 2 of *Treatise of Human Nature*, III, in H. D. Aiken, ed., *Hume's Moral and Political Philosophy* (New York: Hafner, 1948).

15. *Principia Ethica* (Cambridge: Cambridge University Press, 1903).

16. In *God in the Dock* (Grand Rapids: Eerdmans, 1970), 287-300.

ethical thinkers to consider certain actions intrinsically wrong and others intrinsically praiseworthy, apart from judgments about the general happiness of society. Christians especially can appreciate this affirmation of moral absolutes.

But there is a major problem in deontologism as well, that of identifying the absolute, self-attesting moral principles. Plato attempted to do it by means of his general arguments for the existence of the world of forms. But even granting those controversial assertions, we must note that Plato's "Good" was at best an abstraction, a generality incapable of prescribing human duties in concrete situations. Kant tried to establish his catalogue of duties by logical analysis of ethical concepts. An action is obligatory, he said, when I can prescribe it for all persons equally without logical contradiction. But few would agree today that logic alone will distinguish between ethical good and evil in the absence of any empirical or subjective premises.[17]

MIXED SECULAR APPROACHES

The three approaches described above are, I think, the only substantial alternatives available to non-Christian ethicists. Most others will boil down to one of these, or some combination of them.

It is sometimes thought that while a "pure" deontologism, teleologism, or existentialism will not work, some

17. See, for example, Alasdair MacIntyre's critique of "the logical emptiness" of Kant's criterion of the categorical imperative, A Short History of Ethics (New York: Macmillan, 1966).

combination of these may be adequate. Certainly we must have some initial sympathy for this project, for as I shall argue later, the biblical approach is essentially multi-perspectival. Why not a secular multiperspectivalism?

The greatest ethical thinkers, those who had the best sense of the problematics of the "pure" positions, generally held mixed positions. I have mentioned that Plato, who was generally deontologist, included some elements of existentialism. His forms are derived from self-knowledge, the Socratic "know thyself." Similarly Kant's moral law is essentially existential in origin—the moral self telling itself what to do. For him, as for Hegel, the good will is the only thing in the world that is unconditionally good. How, then, does Kant avoid the problems of existentialism? Why *ought* I to obey the voice of the moral law, which is essentially my own voice? Is there really an objective moral law after all? I doubt that there is any adequate answer in Kant to these questions.

Then there is the case of Henry Sidgwick, the nineteenth-century thinker who despite his utilitarianism recognized the danger that a pure utilitarianism could lead to the slaughter of minorities and so on. So he supplemented his utilitarianism with a "principle of justice." Not only should we seek the "greatest good for the greatest number," but we should seek also an equal distribution of happiness. But why? At this point Sidgwick resorts to deontologism—a kind of intuition of what is right. But that introduces the problems of deontologism and robs us of the apparent simplicity and practicality, the perceived benefits of utilitarianism.[18]

G. E. Moore, who coined the phrase "naturalistic fallacy," believed that the ends or goals of ethics had to be learned

18. Sidgwick, *The Methods of Ethics* (New York, Dover, 1966).

along deontological lines—nonempirically, by way of what Moore called "intuition." What of the means to those ends or goals? Here Moore, evidently, was satisfied with utilitarianism and taught that one simply seeks the most efficient means of reaching the deontological goal. Others however, argued that this combination of deontologism with teleologism is unworkable since it reintroduces the problem of the end justifying any means whatsoever. These critics of Moore sought to be more consistent deontologists, but without, I think, escaping the problems I earlier ascribed to consistent deontologism.[19]

Certainly I have not given an exhaustive survey of ethical options, but I have presented the general lines of a critique that will prove plausible to those who are acquainted with this literature and that will apply to most if not all forms of non-Christian ethical systems. I have presented fairly "standard" criticisms of these systems, criticisms made by others before me. But when we put all these criticisms together, they suggest that some radical departure is needed, rather than some mere reworking or recombining of the same ideas.

CHRISTIAN ETHICS

Before I present a positive Christian alternative, let me try to diagnose, from a Christian point of view, the reason why secular ethics is regularly led down such blind alleys. The main problem is not just conceptual confusion or lack of logical skill, nor ignorance of facts, though such problems do

19. One such critic was H. A. Prichard. See his *Moral Obligation* (Oxford: Oxford University Press, 1949).

exist in both Christian and non-Christian ethical systems. The chief problem is rather unbelief itself. Secular ethics, like secular epistemology, seeks to find an absolute somewhere other than in the word of God. It therefore seeks its ethical standard in the most probable locations: human subjectivity (existentialism), the empirical world (teleologism), logic or reason (deontologism). Seeking truth in those locations is not entirely wrong; as we shall see, one who looks *faithfully* in those places will find the word of God, which *is* an adequate ethical standard. And what truth exists in secular ethics exists because, despite its meta-ethic, it has encountered God's word in the self, the world, and the realm of norms (Rom. 1:32). But the secularist is forced to reconcile what he finds in these three realms with his fundamental atheism, and herein the difficulties begin. For if God doesn't exist, what assurance do we have that self, world, and law will tell us the same things? On a theistic basis, God creates the human self and the world to exist together in harmony; and he reveals his own law as the law by which self and world will find fulfillment. But on a nontheistic basis, there is no reason to suppose that self, world, and law will peacefully coexist, or that ethical judgments derived from one source will necessarily cohere with ethical judgments derived from the other two. Indeed, on such a basis, there is every reason to expect that these supposed sources of ethical knowledge will *not* be mutually consistent, and that therefore one must choose which of the three to accept unconditionally. Those who reject God, in other words, must find an alternate source of absolute truth, a substitute god, an idol. But different people prefer different idols. Hence all the confusion.

My positive Christian alternative should be evident by now. A fully Christian ethic accepts as final only God's word.

51

covenant
self
world

That word is found pre-eminently in Scripture, the covenant constitution of the people of God (Deut. 6:6-9; Matt. 5:17-20; II Tim. 3:15-17; II Pet. 1:21), but is also revealed in the world (Ps. 19:1ff.; Rom. 1:18ff.) and in the self (Gen. 1:27ff.; 9:6; Eph. 4:24; Col. 3:10). A Christian will study these three realms presupposing their coherence and therefore seeking at each point to integrate each source of knowledge with the other two.

1. THE EXISTENTIAL PERSPECTIVE

A Christian ethical study of the self will proceed in the light of Scripture and with a recognition of the world as our God-created environment. A Christian will, as in the existential tradition, seek an ethic that realizes human nature and human freedom at their best. But through Scripture he will be able to judge what in human nature is the result of sin and what expresses God's image. This sort of ethical study I describe as coming from the "existential perspective." It is existential in focus, but it does not seek to isolate the self from other sources of God's revelation. Rather it treats the self as a "perspective," a vantage point or angle of vision, from which to view the full range of ethical norms and data. It does justice to the subjective side of human life, particularly our sense of the direct presence of God in his Holy Spirit, recreating us to know and to reflect his holiness. But it does not result in skepticism, because it is anchored in the objectivity of God's word.

2. THE SITUATIONAL PERSPECTIVE

Similarly, a Christian may study the created world, observing the patterns of cause and effect that produce pleasures and pains of different sorts. He must not be blind to

52

that, for Christ calls him to love others as himself. He cares whether people are in pain or having pleasure. But he will carry out this study in the light of scriptural norms (thus escaping the problems of the naturalistic fallacy and of cruelty to minorities, which trap the secular utilitarians) and of his own subjectivity. This sort of study I describe as being from the "situational perspective." It examines the situation as the milieu into which God's norms are to be applied.

3. THE NORMATIVE PERSPECTIVE

And of course a Christian may study God's law in a more direct way, focusing on Scripture itself. But to determine what Scripture says about a particular ethical problem, we must know more than the text of Scripture. To know what Scripture says about abortion, we must know something about abortion. To know what Scripture says about nuclear weapons, we must know something about nuclear weapons. So, odd as it may sound, we cannot know what Scripture says without knowing at the same time something of God's revelation outside of Scripture. And so this sort of study is also a "perspective"—the "normative perspective"—for even when we study the Bible we don't study only the Bible, but we seek to relate the biblical texts to situations and to human subjectivity. We may call this a "Christian deontologism" if we like, but it does not face the difficulties of a secular deontologism. Rather than arbitrarily postulating moral rules or trying futilely to derive them from logical analysis, a Christian ethic accepts God's moral law as an aspect of God's revelation, for the same reasons that he accepts that revelation as God's word.

In each perspective, then, we study all the data available, all the revelation of God. It is not that we study some under the existential perspective, other data under the situational, and still something else under the normative. Rather, in each sort of study we study everything, but with a particular emphasis or focus. The term "perspective" describes well this concept of emphasizing or focusing.

Put in more practical terms, all of this means that when we face an ethical problem, or when we are counselling someone else, we need to ask three questions: (1) What is the problem? (situational perspective); (2) What does Scripture say about it? (normative perspective); and (3) What changes are needed in me (him, her), so that I (he, she) may do the right thing? (existential perspective). Each of those questions must be asked and answered seriously and carefully. And it should be evident that none of those three questions can be fully answered unless we have some answer to the others.

SOME APPLICATIONS

Put this way, it sounds simple enough. And yet this scheme also helps us to see why ethical questions often become difficult. For ethical judgments involve various sorts of knowledge—exegetical, empirical, and psychological—which in turn employ logic and other skills. Since different Christians have different gifts, we need to work together. Not only professional theologians, but Christians of all walks of life need to help in the ethical enterprise. There is much to do and, unlike the situation in secular ethics, much hope for success.

Thus the Scriptures provide us with a meta-ethic that avoids the traps of the various secular ethical positions. This fact has obvious apologetic significance. Not only philosophers, but nonphilosophers, as well, are searching today for ethical stability. We are living at a time when ethical issues are among the most widely discussed topics of interest. A Christian addressing ethical problems can easily get a hearing from people who otherwise have no interest in Christian theology. But most people have no clarity as to how ethical decisions ought to be made; most flounder around amid half-baked versions of existentialism, teleologism, and deontologism. And many fear that beneath all this debate there may not be any substantial basis for ethical certainty. We can help them and show them that in this matter as well as others, the treasures of wisdom and knowledge are found in Christ.

Our meta-ethic also has value within the Christian community as we seek to edify one another in the Lord. Christians, too, need greater clarity on the basis of ethical certainty. Some would admit to having no consistent view of ethics at all; and among those who think they have a consistent view, there is disagreement over what that view should be. Those in the Reformed tradition, especially the theonomic wing, tend to see the law of God in Scripture as the one source of ethical knowledge. Dispensationalists, charismatics, and others (I realize these are strange bedfellows) fear that an emphasis on law will lead to legalism, and thus they tend to develop dangerously subjective notions of divine guidance. Two other groups find the source of ethical certainty in the historical "situation": (1) those oriented toward "biblical theology" or "redemptive history," who find their authority not in Scripture itself but in the events Scripture describes, and (2) those who seek to find God's leading in present-day events (one extreme variety of this tendency being liberation theology).

The view that I am presenting, however, has ecumenical implications; for it helps us to listen to one another and to see both the insights and the limitations of the common views. Yes, the scriptural word is primary as the covenant constitution of the people of God. Yes, we cannot properly use the Scriptures without the subjective illumination of God's Spirit. Yes, Scripture is meaningless unless it is applicable to situations, and so we must indeed understand the times in which we are living. No, none of these perspectives, rightly understood, takes precedence over the other two, because each includes the other two.

In a seminary like Trinity, where many varieties of evangelical theology are represented, you have a great opportunity to observe different "perspectives" on the wonderfully rich gospel God has given us in the Scriptures. If you open your ears and your heart, you can have a rich experience, benefiting from the viewpoints of Christians from traditions other than your own. Of course, sometimes you may hear or read viewpoints that don't deserve to be called "perspectives," but rather are simply wrong. Still, I commend to you an attitude of openness with a slight wariness (rather than the reverse). You do not need to fear that openness will dissolve into relativism, because God's word, the covenant constitution of his people, stands firm. Hear the viewpoints of your classmates and professors, but hear God's word most of all.

SCRIPTURE INDEX

57

59

60

GENERAL INDEX